Dear Graduate

LETTERS
of
PRACTICAL
ADVICE
from

Don Wilkerson

A Special Gift

PRESENTED TO

FROM

DATE

Letters

1. Just for You...page 5

2. Coming Down Off the Mountain...page 11

3. Facing the Future...page 17

4. Stop and Ask for Directions...page 21

5. Church Life...page 27

6. Practical Advice...page 33

7. My Top Ten Sentence Sermons...page 39

8. Don't Give Up Your Testimony...page 45

9. Growing to the Next Level...page 51

10. When Loneliness Strikes...page 57

11. A Solemn Warning...page 63

12. Go Forth!...page 69

Dear Graduate

Letter One

Just for You!

***Congratulations,
You made it!***

You know, of course,
God is the One who
made it happen.
To Him belongs
all the glory.

Don Wilkerson

As the saying goes—give credit where credit is due. You are to be commended for your faith, perseverance, discipline, and obedience in completing what has been a great challenge.

Now you are ready for the next step. Your graduation should be a day to remember. Whenever in the days to come you are discouraged, ready to give up, or under Satanic attack—point back to this day. God did it! You made it through the program. Even as the children of Israel were always to remember the miracle crossing of the Red Sea and their deliverance from Egypt, so you should mark this day as having reached the other side towards the Promised Land of your full inheritance in Christ.

The next phase of your Christian walk awaits you—with all its opportunities, tests, and possibilities. Whether you are planning on starting a new career, working in the ministry, furthering your education, returning home, or choosing some new path, always remember this: God has brought you this far, and He wants to complete what He began.

It took a miracle to bring you to this place of victory. It will take many more small and large miracles to be succe ssful in the next phase of your spiritual journey.

"I will do a new thing."

Someone has said, "I like the dreams of the future, rather than the history of the past" (before knowing Christ). Always remember Isaiah 43:18-19, "But forget all that—it is nothing compared to what I am going to do. For I am about to do a brand-new thing. Do you not see I have already begun? I will make a pathway through the wilderness for my people to come home. I will create rivers for them in the desert!" (NLT)

"Remember ye not the former things, neither consider the things of old. Behold, I will do a new thing" (KJV). God has done many new things for you, things you and others never thought possible. If God did it

Don Wilkerson

during the days of your recovery and rehabilitation, He can do it in the days to come, no matter what challenges you face.

This book is specially prepared just for you, to remind you where you have come from and where God wants to take you. The Scriptures, quotations, writings, and words of wisdom have been selected for your inspiration and instruction. Hopefully, in the days to come, you can refer back again and again to this for encouragement. May this book always be a reminder of this special occasion when you received your Certificate of Completion of God's program that helped change your life.

Just For You

~ Milestones ~

_____

New Birth

_____

Completed Program

~ Other Important Dates ~

_____

_____

_____

_____

Dear Graduate

Letter Two

Coming Down...

...off the Mountain

*W*herever you graduate from, it can be said that you are coming down off the 'mountain.'

A mountain in Scripture is a type of place where you have enjoyed a spiritual "high." A place of blessing and being in the presence of God. You are coming down off a spiritual, maybe even a literal mountain. It has been a place of training, correction, inspiration, and yes, testings and difficulties.

You have had the advantage of a protective environment. You've been told when to get up, when to retire, when to study, when to work, play, or go here or there and do this, that and the other. You're probably ready–more than ready–to enjoy freedom from rules and regulations.

Or are you?

The community you have been a part of for the past months or year, you will now have to be separated from. Some graduates do not make the adjustment to being outside a protective environment. It's important to realize the coming down off the mountain can be a step forward, and not backward. You do not have to fail or fall. The same God and Lord Who was with you on the mountain will be with you in the valley, the plains, or wherever you go–if you keep the faith and have a positive attitude.

You have to make character.

Now it's time to move on. Even if you remain as a worker, you are still moving on from one stage of your spiritual journey to another. It is time to add on to your spiritual development.

2 Peter 1:5 says, "Make every effort to... add to your faith."

Peter says we have inherited the Divine nature of Christ, but that we must give attention to our part of Christian growth. Add to what you have learned. Add to your character. No one is born either naturally or supernaturally with character. You have to make character.

It is in the adding that is difficult. Some graduates do not add on when they come down off the mountain. They try to live on yesterday's bread. It never works.

God is not just God of the mountains. Remember as someone has said, "Wherever you go–there you are." And, wherever you go, God is there. But you must stay connected to Him, His word, and His people and continue to do His will.

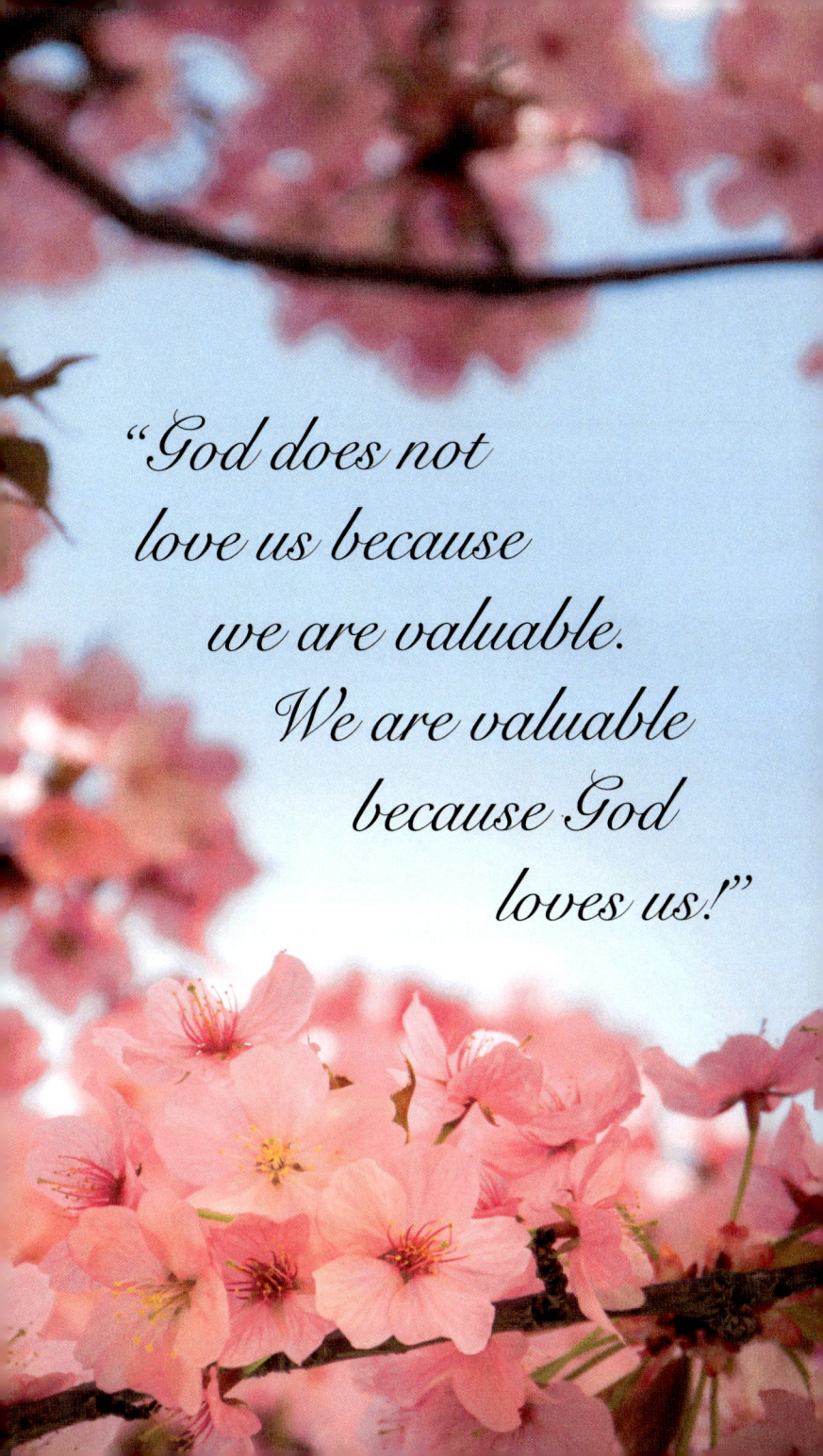

"God does not love us because we are valuable. We are valuable because God loves us!"

Dear Graduate

Letter Three

Facing the Future

"You have not passed this way before."

Joshua 3:4

Many people are fearful when they face the future. Perhaps you are too; for you have "never been there before." That's what can be so unsettling about tomorrow. We go down paths we've never been on before.

Don Wilkerson

If on the occasion of your transition from program to reentry you're very fearful, or just some what fearful, I for one am glad. There are unhealthy fears and healthy fears. An unhealthy fear is when we become so paralyzed about the future we don't make good decisions. A healthy fear is when we realize that we cannot lean on our own understanding and that we must always depend on the Lord in all things.

God wants you to succeed!

Self-confidence is good up to a point, but if it means we leave God out of our planning and our decisions, it can lead to failure.

Go forward into your tomorrows with caution, with a kind of fear that causes you to lean strong on the Lord for every decision and for each new day you face.

If you are anxious about the future then listen to God's Word and take courage.

Facing the Future

Jesus said, "I will never leave you nor forsake you" (Hebrews 13:5). "The Lord is my shepherd; I shall not want...He leads me in the paths of righteousness for His name's sake" (Psalm 23:1, 3).

God wants you to succeed more than you do. After all, His name is at stake in all that you do. When you are victorious, Christ is honored and glorified. When you fail, the devil gets a victory.

"You have not passed this way before," but God goes before you to make the path safe, secure, and satisfying.

Dear Graduate

Letter Four

Stop and Ask...

...for Directions

When driving to a place I've never been before and I get lost, I hate to ask for directions. It really upsets my wife. I've learned it's typical of men. We hate to stop and ask for directions.

Don Wilkerson

I ask myself—why am I this way? I have a few insights on this: One. I don't like to admit I'm lost. Two. I think I can eventually find my way. Three. At the root of numbers one and two is pride. (Those of you raised with cell phones and google maps are wondering why I'd ever get lost!)

In life and in spiritual matters however, I try always to stop and ask God directions.

In my research for this book I read various other books addressed to graduates. In one entitled "Where Ya Gonna Go?" I found the following sound advice relative to asking and trusting God for guidance and direction in your life. Author Kevin Johnson writes: "God wants to show you where to go—but even your understanding of what He wants may be incomplete.

Picture this: driving on a country road on a move this night. Your headlights

Stop and Ask for Directions

brighten the road one hundred feet in front of you, but you're driving fast enough that even if you slammed on the brakes, it would take two hundred feet to stop. You can't see as far ahead as you need to. You may know that's called "overdriving your headlights." It's scary. You're cheese-spread if a deer leaps in front of you or a curve comes up fast.

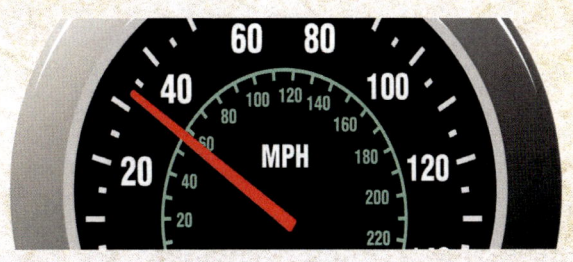

You probably want to drive your life with your foot to the floor; to push forward. You want God to tell you exactly what your future holds so you can get there fast. But driving faster than God chooses to give you guidance is like plunging stupidly into the darkness.

Slow down. You won't waste your life if you live in God's Way, God's pace. "Be strong and take heart and wait for the Lord" (Psalm 27:14).

If you constantly asked a friend for directions to her house, but always took your own route and then complain about getting lost, she would give up trying to tell you the way. Likewise, God knows that unless you're ready to listen and obey, showing you the truth is useless.

God enthusiastically gives wisdom to anyone who asks (See James 1:5). He expects you to trust His desire and ability to answer your requests. He expects you to believe Him enough to act on the truth He shows you—to follow His directions; to walk His way, to do what He says.

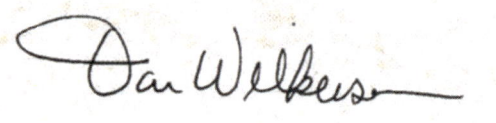

"The will of God will not take you where the grace of God cannot keep you."

Dear Graduate

Letter Five

Church Life

You've been taught the importance of joining a church and participating in church life. Now it's time to put this into practice.

You may have come from a church and will probably go back to it. If this is the case, here's some practical advice. Don't compare your church with the program. Learn what the church can do for you, and what it can't. Remember, don't depend just

Don't depend just on church for your spiritual growth.

on the church for your spiritual growth. Have your own personal, private time with God.

If you have not chosen a church, here is some advice that applies to anyone choosing and going to a church.

Connect with the body. Make friendships in the church. One good way is to get involved in a small group, if they don't have one, or join some other group in the church. This is so you can get closer to people and build meaningful relationships.

Find a mentor. Let the Lord lead you to someone you can talk to when needed. Finding a mentor does not mean you have to necessarily ask someone to be your mentor (that may scare them off); but you can pick out someone to get to know and over time perhaps a relationship can develop in which you can share problems, needs, and prayer requests.

If you're checking out several churches to see which one to attend, choose one that has good preaching, teaching, and worship; the church that has good 'body life.' This means a church that has the kind of activities where people get to know each other and build good relationships. I once asked a graduate, "How is the church you're attending? He said, "Oh, it's an in-and-out church." So I asked him, "What do you mean?" He explained that he went in and he enjoyed the service, but when the service was over, that was all there was.

There was no outreach. No small groups. No way of getting to know and connect with the church family. Find a church that is more than *Sunday-go-to-meeting*. You have known what 24/7 Christianity is all about. You need a church that is more than the one or two day a week kind of church.

Martin Luther said this about the church: "Now the church is not wood and stone, but the company of people who believe in Christ. Anyone who is to find Christ must first find the church. How could anyone know where Christ is and what faith is unless he knows where His believers are."

> *"God does not give us overcoming life. He gives us life as we overcome."*

Dear Graduate

Letter Six

Practical Advice

It's been my experience with graduates (from any school or program) that they often worry unnecessarily, blow things out of proportion, and get too stressed out over the wrong things.

Don Wilkerson

You may or may not have been given some practical advice about some things you need to do in a life beyond the voluntary confinement of a residential discipleship program. In a book entitled *"The Don't Sweat Guide for Graduates,"* author Richard Carlson, Ph.D. lists 100 practical ideas for graduates. I'll list just 12 of them for you:

1. Appearance is important for confidence. For most employers, first impressions are lasting impressions.

2. Know that job openings always come up. If you're turned down for a job, don't get discouraged. There are more opportunities out there, if you look for them.

3. Take notes when learning new task. The best way to learn on the job is the same way you learned in classes take notes.

4. Reorganize your time. Think logically about the time you have. And then in your off work hours, find a way to fit in your spiritual life while still getting the practical things done (shopping, checking emails, paying bills).

Practical Advice

5. Accept that you will make mistakes. Mistakes are part of life. Everyone makes them, even your boss. No matter how hard you try, no matter how many notes you've taken or how well you understand a procedure; one day something will fall through the cracks. It's how you deal with it that is most important.

6. Ignore office (work) gossip. People use it to complain and the complaint can get in your spirit, doing more harm than good. Listen politely and walk away. The offenders will soon learn you're not a garbage can for the gossip.

7. Don't be put off by real-world responsibilities. You have already taken on a lot of real world responsibilities without knowing it. However, you're going to face a lot of unexpected and unwanted stuff. Just remember, it's what everyone has to face.

every day. The more you face it, the stronger you will be able to handle whatever comes your way.

8. Save a little money each week. Don't make the mistake of thinking you can't save at least a little each week. You can if you discipline your wants. Save for the future. You'll be so glad you did. Savings is the best money you don't spend.

9. Don't spend money on things you really don't need. This could be a challenge you face the rest of your life.

People get into heavy debt, even ruin their lives by uncontrolled spending. Meet your needs first, then if you have the funds, take care of your wants.

Being on your own gives you a wonderful sense of freedom but if you spend money on things you don't need, that freedom can soon become a bondage.

Practical Advice

10. Don't worry if you don't like your first job. Here's a newsflash: in all likelihood, your first job would not be your last job or your only job–whether you're working in a ministry or secular job. So if you're not thrilled with it and it's not all you hoped it would be, don't worry. You won't be at this job forever.

11. Set up a budget. You may want to get help from someone who operates with a budget. Be careful who you ask. A lot of people don't budget well. Find a good financial consultant and I don't mean a professional. I recommend the book from which the above is quoted.

12. Be open and teachable. Depending on your age and background you may have already held good jobs. But remember you're starting all over again, and even if you've been successful in the work world in the past, you need to approach life as a newcomer and be open to practical advice.

Dear Graduate

Letter Seven

My Top Ten...

...Sentence Sermons

Top ten lists are popular today—so I have my own list! These nuggets of truth are selected to help you think about issues you will certainly face in the future, and to encourge you towards a successful spiritual journey.

I have preached at many graduation ceremonies just like yours. How I wish I could have spoken at your graduation. Those who know me know how I love to preach. Since I could not be at your graduation, this book gives me an opportunity to speak to you in another way. If I were able to preach to you, I might develop an entire message out of one of the sentence sermons that follows. Here are my top ten one-liner sermons. (Note the words of wisdom that are contained in these ten sayings I have selected for you.)

1. The best thing about the future is that it comes only one day at a time. "Don't be anxious about tomorrow. God will take care of your tomorrow's too. Live one day at a time" (Matthew 6:34, TLB).

2. No sin is so small that it should be swept under the rug. "I am troubled by my sin" (Psalm 38:18).

3. Courage is fear that has said its prayers. "I have told you these things, so that in Me you may have peace. In this world you'll have trouble. But take heart! I have overcome the world" (John 16:33).

4. God does not love us because we are valuable. We are valuable because he loves us. "The Lord delights in those that fear Him, who put their hope in His unfailing love" (Psalm 147:11).

5. If God sends us on stony paths, He will provide us with strong shoes. "Be strong and let us fight bravely for our people and the cities of our God. The Lord will do what is good in His sight" (2 Samuel 10:12).

6. Never be afraid to trust an unknown future to a known God. "I will turn the darkness into light before them and make the rough places smooth" (Isaiah 42:16).

7. There is no right way to do the wrong thing. "There is a way that seems right to a man, but in the end it leads to death" (Proverbs 14:12).

8. It is better to keep one's mouth shut and be thought a fool than to open it and resolve all doubt. "When words are many, sin is not absent, but he who holds his tongue is wise" (Proverbs 10:19).

9. A mind grows by what it feeds on. "The mind controlled by the Spirit is life and peace" (Romans 8:6).

10. Success consists in getting up more times than you fall. "My foes will rejoice when I fall. But I trust in Your unfailing love" (Psalm 13:4-5).

I suppose I could preach a whole sermon on each of the above insightful truths. May the Holy Spirit take these power point words and make them real to your heart.

"What we do does not shape who we are.

Who we are shapes what we do."

Dear Graduate

Letter Eight

Don't Give Up...

...Your Testimony

"All my friends are waiting for me to slip."

Jeremiah 20:10

A testimony is NOT JUST what you stand up to give in a church service or outside doing street evangelism. It's what you are outside of church.

Whether you give your testimony before one person, ten persons, hundreds of people or thousands; in the eyes of God, what you say and what you tell is only true and valid by how you live for Christ when no one is watching.

How do you live when no one is watching?

Proverbs 21:1, "A good name is rather to be chosen than great riches, and loving favor rather than silver and gold." There is no amount of money I would exchange for a *good name*. A *good name* is the same as having a good testimony. Loving favor of our heavenly Father is bestowed upon us when we have the reputation among those who know us best of having a *good name.*

If someone mentions the name of another person to you, I guarantee that you will immediately think of something about that person. It may be good, or maybe bad. We all have a given earthly name, and we all have a name, a label, which we acquire by the way we talk, act, and live.

Don't Give Up Your Testimony

Some of you have had an awful name in your past that you have had to overcome, and may still be trying to overcome. Your name may have once been a shame to you, to your family, even to your neighborhood. We have an expression in America that says, "a persons name is mud"—a derogatory term. This originated from the name Dr. Mudd who treated John Wilkes Booth, the assassin of Abraham Lincoln. Sometimes it's hard to live down once we acquire a bad name.

Some of you had a name that was a lot worse than mud or dirt, but God has cleansed your life and your reputation. Like Abram and Jacob of old, you have been given a new name—a *good name!*

The worst thing you could ever do when you've been given a new name (because of a new life) is to lose that *good name.*

Don't give up your testimony!

Note Proverbs 22:1 says, "A good name is rather to be chosen...than great riches." We do not acquire a *good name* by chance, by accident, or by manipulation. You cannot buy a *good name* like companies that pay millions of dollars to acquire a good name for their business or product. You have to choose to have a good testimony. It is both a work of grace and commitment and effort on your part.

I have seen converts lose their testimony in one night of temptation; they chose drugs and the flesh instead of the Spirit of God, or they chose a few hours or a few moments in bed with someone and by one foolish choice, their *good name* and their testimony were ruined.

Choosing a *good name* means you exercise discernment between what is false and what is true–and you bear testimony to the truth. The word 'choose' or 'chosen' in Hebrew means "select, distinguish, love, like to be pleasing."

Don't Give Up Your Testimony

Life is like a giant supermarket that offers good fruit and bad fruit. You can load your shopping basket with junk or jewels—with garbage or blessings. You make the choice, and when you do, your *good name* is either increased or it dies.

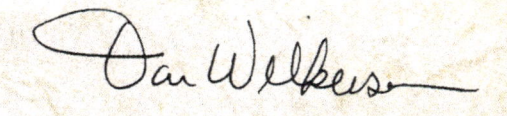

Dear Graduate

Letter Nine

Growing...

...to the Next Level

Celebration can turn into disaster if you say, "Now I'm free. My time is my own. My decisions are my own. My future is my own."

The most dangerous time in anyone's life is right after completing school, a program, or some other milestone. Such a time is for celebration. However, celebration can turn into a disaster if you say, "Now I'm free. My time is my own. My decisions are my own. My future is my own."

You are right—and you are wrong!

Yes, you've earned the right to your diploma or Graduation Certificate. You have earned the right to move onto set your own schedule and make your own decisions. Yet you are not your own. You've been "bought with a price." Why would God do all He has done for you to now let you do your own thing?

No, it's time to move to the next level. If you do not continue to grow spiritually, emotionally, and mentally, you will die. And from where you came from, dying can mean just that. Your journey with Christ has reached the level of a new beginning. Will you step up or down? Will you go forward, or backward?

My friend Steve Hill was a well-known American evangelist and graduate of Teen Challenge. He wrote a daily devotional entitled "Daily Awakenings."

Here is the devotion for June 10th, based on Romans 6:11,12: Likewise reckon you also yourselves to be dead indeed to sin, but also alive unto God through Jesus Christ our Lord. Let not sin therefore reign in your mortal body, that ye should obey it in the lusts thereof.

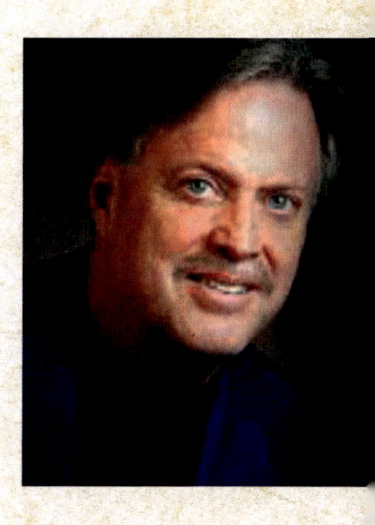

Steve wrote: "Christianity is a life change—a continual life change. In the example of Christ we have been given a goal at which to aim, and as Charles Finney explains, it is that aim which distinguishes a true follower of Christ. Aim at being perfect. Every young convert should be taught that if it is not his purpose to live without sin, he has not yet begun to be a Christian. What is Christianity but supreme love of God and a supreme purpose of heart or disposition to obey God. If there is not this, there is no Christianity at all. It should be our constant purpose (aim) to live wholly to God and obey all His commandments. We should live so that if we were to sin, it would be an inconsistency, an exception, an individual case in which we act contrary to the fixed purpose of our lives.

That is the essence of the true Christian walk; not to see what we can get away with, but instead, to see what we can stay away from. In following that course, it is easier to live a holy life, focused on our example—Jesus."

This is a wise challenge from the late Steve Hill. He's been there—a graduate that had to make a decision to "grow to the next level." Let your aim be to go higher and be perfected in Christ.

"No one is born either naturally or supernaturally with character. You have to make character."

Dear Graduate

Letter Ten

When Loneliness...

...Strikes

I used to think loneliness was a girl thing; not a guy thing.
I was wrong.
Loneliness can strike at the strangest times.

I have known the loneliness in long absences away from my family, the loneliness when heavy decisions weigh on me, as well as other times.

You will face such times as you adjust to new places, new people, and new challenges. These can be times of serious danger, or opportunities to draw closer to the Lord. Many a person has fallen into sin (sexual immorality) in times of loneliness of relationships (with the opposite sex).

The loneliness of boredom can lead to drinking, drugs or other fleshly expressions of sin.

You should beware that times of loneliness may strike—be prepared to to work through it successfully. How can this be done? Recognize that emotions can be tricky. One minute you're on top of a mountain, and the next you're down deep in a valley. When face-to-face with loneliness, don't get stuck in a negative emotion. Keep a positive perspective and evaluate your situation.

If you ride out your emotions on a downward swing, always remember, tomorrow can be a better day.

Do something to rise up out of the discouragement and possible defeat that can result from loneliness. Ask yourself these questions: What is the source of my loneliness? Is it physical, spiritual, circumstantial (away from home, taking on a new challenge)?

Loneliness is an opportunity to draw close to the Lord.

Is there a deep-seated issue from the past you have not dealt with? You may be experiencing something deeper than loneliness. It could be depression and you do not even know it. This may require pastoral counseling.

Whatever the source of our loneliness, it is an opportunity to draw closer to the Lord. Read the Psalms. Note the times of

David's loneliness and how he drew closer to the Lord at such times.

C.S. Lewis said in one of his writings: "The time will come when you will regard all this misery as a small price to pay for having been brought to that dependence. Meanwhile the trouble is that relying on God has to begin all over again every day as if nothing has been done yet."

Connect with Christ when loneliness strikes. Pour out your heart and tell Jesus everything you're feeling—everything! Tell Him when or if you're angry, jealous, or fearful. Don't worry, nothing you tell Jesus will shock Him or make Him love you less. He sympathizes with our weaknesses (Hebrews 4:15). The fact of the matter is that it's okay to be lonely at times.

When Loneliness Strikes

There's a lot to be learned when you're alone. Besides getting to know the Lord better, you can get to know yourself better. You might even come to enjoy alone times.

When you've take in some of the above steps to work through and come up out of loneliness, here are some other practical suggestions:

    Read a book
    Walk through a mall
    Start a journal
    Write a poem
    Call a trustworthy friend
    Treat yourself to a chocolate sundae
    Go jogging or work out

However, the above suggestions should be done only after taking some spiritual steps to deal with loneliness. Remember what Jesus says: "I will not leave you orphans; I will come to you" (John 14:18).

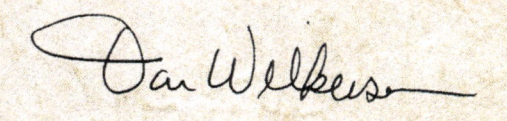

Dear Graduate

Letter Eleven

A Solemn Warning

I have seen too many graduates fall immediately, or soon after graduation. I've asked myself why? After analyzing this for years, there are some observations I need to share with you.

Don Wilkerson

Reasons why graduates fall!

1. They have no fear of God.

If you do not walk holy and reverent before God, which is what a wholesome fear of God is, it would have been better if you never were in a program to begin with. To whom much is given, much is required. To sin against the Light is one of the worst sins one can commit. If you willfully turn your back on Christ, if you think things were bad in your life before your accepted Him, look out. All hell is going to break loose in your life.

It's about eternity!

2. Going through the program without the program going through you.

Let's face it, you may have adjusted to the program real good—without being real. You've been faking it a lot. Maybe you have been an environmental Christian. In other words, the environment dictated you act a

A Solemn Warning

certain way, and you have been a good actor. You went to the program but the program's purpose, teaching, training and discipline have not really penetrated deeply inside you.

Now you may have to pay for just 'doing time.' I hope you stay clean. Most who are as I am describing fall sooner rather than later. You may be the exception and stay clean. But what does it profit a man, or woman, or youth to get a graduation certificate yet lose his/ her own soul. The program is not just about getting clean or staying clean. It's about eternity. It's about heaven—or hell.

It's not too late to choose.

3. No goals! No plans!

It's never too late to establish goals. By now you should have defined, through prayer and the counsel of others, some short-term goals.
If not, do so immediately.

If you don't know where you're going, any road will get you there. Perhaps you just slid through the program.

The reason for having no goals sometimes comes down to spiritual laziness. It's wake-up time. The world awaits you with all it's potential dangers, but also opportunities. Clear your mind of "can't."

The reason some do not have goals is because of fear—the fear of failure. Put your mind in positive gear, set your heart in a faith mode and ask God to open His door for you. As small and insignificant as the door may seem, go through it and watch bigger and better doors open for you.

You may be disappointed if you fail, but you are doomed if you don't try. "The sluggard craves and gets nothing, but the desires of the diligent are fully satisfied" (Proverbs 13:4).

If any or all of these things describe you, what can you do now that you're graduating?

1. Get serious with God!

2. Get into a church where you can study God's Word seriously.

3. Get on your knees and ask God to show you now what to do with your life.

Dan Wilkerson

Dear Graduate

Letter Twelve

Go Forth!

God stands fast as your Rock, steadfast as your Safeguard, sleepless as your Watcher, valiant as your Champion!

—Charles Spurgeon

Don Wilkerson

A final word of encouragement and congratulations! You have joined one of the most remarkable alumni groups of any institution in the world. Your graduation ranks higher, in my estimation, than if you had graduated from Harvard, Yale or some other prestigious university.

You have graduated from:

***Death to Life!
Darkness to Light!
Slavery to Freedom!
Hopelessness to Hope!***

Never be ashamed of the fact you have gone through and completed a faith-based recovery program. You don't need to wear label that says you are "x" this or "x" that. However, whenever you have the opportunity to share your testimony—don't hold back.

"For I live in eager expectation and hope that I will never do anything that causes me shame, but that I will always be bold for Christ, as I have been in the past, and that my life will honor Christ, whether I live or die. For me living is Christ..." (Philippians 1:20-21, NLT)

Your graduation stands as a challenge to scoffers, skeptics and those that say a cure for addiction and life-controlling problems is not possible. You prove them wrong! God has made you a winner, not a loser.

It's been a special joy to prepare and write these letters to you. All over the world, men, women and youth are being set free and joining the Alumni of the Reclaimed. It is our desire that you, along with your brothers and sisters from other nations, will except this "special edition" book as a treasured keepsake for years to come.

May this gift given to you by those that love and care for you, and have contributed so much to your reaching this victory stage of your life, be kept in a visible place as a future reminder of this Graduation Day and always remember...

...you are Chosen!
1 Peter 2:9

...you are Changed!
2 Corinthians 5:17

...you are Complete!
Philippians 1:6

Prayerfully yours, *Dan Wilkerson*

Go forth in Jesus' Name
Go forth, His Word to proclaim
We are commission to show men the way
Go forth in Jesus' Name

By His Spirit, and the Power of His Might
We will conquer the darkness
with His Glorious Light
Jesus is faithful!
And He'll never change
Go forth in Jesus' Name!

Song by the Brooklyn Tabernacle Choir

About the Author

Don Wilkerson is the Co-founder of Teen Challenge with his brother David. He served 26 years as Director of Brooklyn Teen Challenge. In 1987, he joined his brother David as Co-founder of Times Square Church in Manhattan, New York. In 1995, Don founded Global Teen Challenge, helping to open Teen Challenge centers and train workers worldwide. In 2008, Don was called back to Brooklyn to lead Teen Challenge where he serves as President Emeritus. He has authored 14 books including The Challenge Study Bible, filled with advice and wisdom from over 60 years of frontlines ministry experience.

Dear Graduate - Second Edition, 2020
Copyright by Don Wilkerson
Independently Published
ISBN 9798600750081
www.brooklyntc.org

Made in the USA
Las Vegas, NV
25 March 2025